the

Mother's
Companion

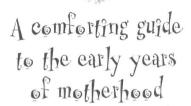

A comforting guide
to the early years
of motherhood

First published in Australia in 1999 by:
Tracy Marsh Publications Pty Ltd

Published in the United States and Canada in 2001 by:
Wildcat Canyon Press
A Division of Circulus Publishing Group, Inc.
2716 Ninth St.
Berkeley, CA 94710 USA
Tel: (888) 774-7595
Fax: (510) 848-1326
Email: info@wildcatcanyon.com

Author: Tracy Marsh
Coauthors: Sharon Hauptberger and Lisa Braver Moss
Editor: Judith Simpson
Designer: Vanessa Byrne
Illustrator: Amanda Upton
Publishing Manager: Jane Moseley
Production Director: Mick Bagnato

ISBN 1 885171 59 5

Produced by:
Tracy Marsh Publications Pty Ltd
PO Box 116, Henley Beach, SA 5022 Australia
Tel: (08) 8355 4716
Fax: (08) 8355 4916
Email: tracy@tracymarsh.com

Manufactured by Phoenix Offset, Hong Kong
Printed in Hong Kong

The suggestions and ideas contained within this book are those of the authors. The authors and publisher do not accept any liability for the opinions, advice or information published in or in relation to this publication.

At the time of publication all the telephone numbers and contact details were correct. However, these could have changed since publication.

Thank you to the following publishers for permission to reproduce quotes used in this book:
HarperCollins Publishers Australia (quotes on pages 14, 26, 80, 95)
Penguin Australia (quotes on pages 6, 98, 110)

Cataloging-in-Publication data is on record at the Library of Congress.

the

Mother's Companion

A comforting guide
to the early years
of motherhood

by Tracy Marsh

with Sharon Hauptberger

& Lisa Braver Moss

WILDCAT CANYON PRESS
A Division of Circulus Publishing Group, Inc.
Berkeley, California

*This book is dedicated to Sophia Isabella,
my beautiful daughter who changed my life forever…*

Contents

God could not be everywhere and therefore he created mothers.

JEWISH PROVERB

Introduction

How to use The Mother's Companion

From birth, your baby will be the focus of everyone's attention. As he/she reaches different developmental milestones, you will find that the first twelve months of life are a time of amazing growth. Your own life, too, changes profoundly and irreversibly during this intense period.

Many books on early parenting are naturally centered on the infant. Often, little attention is given to the parents and, particularly, to the mother who has carried and given birth to this new life. This book is for mothers and describes what mothers may themselves experience during the early years of motherhood.

The Mother's Companion contains note pages for you to record your own experiences. Writing is one of the most effective ways of coping with situations that may be stressful. On these pages, you can record your feelings and keep track of how things are changing. Recording your experiences is also a means of checking which things help or hinder you in your new role.

The primary message of *The Mother's Companion* is that you, as a mother, are changing and growing with your baby. This book will provide you with a useful tool from birth through the early years of new motherhood. It will also be an irreplaceable memento to treasure for the rest of your life.

Keeping records

Keeping a record of your feelings and thoughts serves several purposes. It

- gives you an opportunity to give yourself a pat on the back for a job well done or to let off steam
- gives you time to reflect now and as time passes, allowing you to see how far you've come and to appreciate the confidence and abilities you've gained
- allows you to be more objective — writing is often more constructive than keeping thoughts in your head
- gives time for your feelings to settle when your calm has deserted you or if you're feeling overwhelmed

Don't censor your thoughts. Express yourself without inhibition — this is a safe place to record your experiences. Sometimes your thoughts will come easily; at other times it may seem impossible to think at all! But you will always be able to write something.

Some pages have questions to prompt you. Others are left blank for you to fill in as you wish. Here are some thought-starters.

- How are you feeling at this moment?
- What have you done for yourself since your baby was born?
- Is there something that you're really looking forward to?
- What inspires you? What challenges you?
- List positive thoughts about yourself, your qualities and achievements.

Only a mother knows a mother's fondness.

LADY MARY MONTAGUE

chapter 1

Welcome to Motherhood

Reflections on your pregnancy and birth

Congratulations! Now you're a mother!

Becoming a mother

Becoming a mother, especially for the first time, is a joyous event and something that should be celebrated. Whether you've arrived at this destination by choice or by chance, there's no doubt that the journey you've embarked on will alter your life.

Women today are having fewer children, and often defer motherhood until they have established a foothold in a successful career or, perhaps, have seen something of the world.

Regardless of your age or any other factors, becoming a mother is likely to be one of life's most exciting and challenging undertakings. If you're game enough to return for a second, third, fourth time, you can expect to extend and multiply those challenges and rewards accordingly.

Pregnancy

Obviously, pregnancy is a time of incredible change. It is the first stage in your metamorphosis to becoming a mother. Besides the physical transformation, pregnancy brings about other changes. These are predominantly emotional due to hormonal upheaval. Your partner may have noticed your mood swings even if you haven't!

The Hormone Gremlin

Your emotions tend to reflect your attitude toward the progressing pregnancy. Some women positively glow during this time while others are far from radiant. Anxiety and anticipation are feelings that can be exaggerated by the outcome of any previous pregnancies—terminations, miscarriages and stillbirths, or cot deaths included.

It would be unusual for a mother-to-be not to anticipate what lies ahead. She may have an easy, healthy pregnancy and continue life as normal, or she may experience 24-hour "morning" sickness and other pregnancy-related discomforts causing most of her waking thoughts to revolve around the coming baby. All changes aside, women undergo an amazing personal transformation over the forty weeks or so from conception to birth.

For some women, pregnancy may have been planned, for others, it may have been an accident, unplanned and definitely a surprise or maybe even a shock. For those who have suffered infertility and the subsequent merry-go-round of IVF and other fertility treatments, the pregnancy may be long awaited—the culmination of years of hope and prayers. The focus of pregnancy is, however, usually fixed on the birth. Antenatal classes tend to echo this focus and often provide little practical advice in preparation for parenthood.

The birth

While books and antenatal classes may be informative and educate you as to the theory of birth, nothing—absolutely nothing—can truly prepare a first-time mother for this event. Women with an older child may be surprised to find that their second experience of birth is considerably different from that of the first—possibly more complicated, probably much easier.

You might have anticipated a long, drawn-out labor yet felt confident in your body's ability to give birth. It may be that you imagined a natural, drug-free birth and ended up having your baby delivered by caesarean section. Perhaps you gave the labor little thought and found yourself overwhelmed at the intensity of the pain. Possibly, the contractions were bearable and you anticipated the impending birth positively and with excitement, or maybe you decided that the pain was just too much. Many women switch between extremes from hour to hour and even from minute to minute!

The experience of birth is as individual as that of pregnancy and, again, this varies for each woman for each birth. You cannot compare your experience to other women's birthing experiences.

Sometimes mothers feel that they didn't cope well in labor or they didn't do what they thought they would. Birth is not something that can be definitively planned. You have not failed if things didn't go as you wished. In the long run, what matters most is the outcome—your baby's safe arrival.

Bonding

Once your baby is born, you may begin to wonder why you don't feel anything special and intimate with your baby. When are you going to bond with your baby? Bonding is a term that has been bandied about to varying degrees in recent years. Falling in love with your baby—forming that emotional connection—may take some time. It's not usually instantaneous. Bonding is the formation of a special relationship, with the emphasis on *relationship*. Bonding with your baby is something you both do—he/she with you, as well as you with him/her.

Many mothers feel quite detached following birth. Such emotional indifference may come as a surprise. Don't put pressure on yourself; there is nothing must feel. One day—

The ultimate criteria by which you can judge successful delivery are a healthy mother and baby.
EISENBERG, HATHAWAY, AND MURKOFF, *WHAT TO EXPECT THE FIRST YEAR*

maybe at the hour of birth, maybe three months later—you'll discover an incredibly deep love for and connection with your baby.

A "newborn" mother

Those first few days following birth often pass in a haze. Your feelings might range from exhilaration and elation to exhaustion and everything in between. Some of the discomforts to contend with following birth include:

- a possible episiotomy, tear, or both
- afterpains—when the uterus contracts, beginning to return to its normal size—are felt more strongly while breastfeeding and are usually more intense following each subsequent birth
- maybe pain from the incision of a caesarean section delivery, which is usually more traumatic if performed as an emergency rather than an elective, and especially if performed following a lengthy labor
- hard, hot, swollen, heavy breasts while breast milk is "coming in"

You also have your beautiful newborn to care for. Many hospitals now have 24-hour rooming in, where your baby stays with you from birth. You will learn how to breastfeed or how to sterilize bottles and make up formula preparations, how to change diapers, and how to bathe and handle your baby. Enjoy the peaceful moments you share with your baby. Take the opportunity to just be there and get to know each other.

Some maternity units now offer an opportunity to "debrief" following childbirth. This gives you a chance to reflect on and "re-live" labor and birth, to express your emotions openly and honestly and, thereby, relieve yourself of any negativity about the experience.

When people experience any highly emotional event, good or bad, there is a strong need to share the experience, to have others acknowledge the emotions involved. A new mother may need to talk about the birth and, if so, someone should listen to what she has to say. This is true for women who have had positive birthing experiences as well as for those whose experience has been traumatic.

Following a hospital birth, information sessions or classes are often held for new parents. These include postnatal exercises, physiotherapy, and baby-care basics. Educational videos are usually available on everything from back care to breastfeeding and a multitude of other subjects related to baby management.

Some decisions cannot be made until your baby is born. It is probably a good idea not to anticipate too much or to project too far into the future because you never know what temperament your baby will have or what his/her needs will be, apart from the basics. It is better to say, for example, "I would have preferred to have breastfed" than to say, "I should have breastfed," with all its accompanying guilt.

In those very early postnatal days there is much to learn about your newborn and choices to be made, including whether to:
- breast or bottle feed
- use a pacifier or not
- use disposable or cloth diapers

Every baby is unique. Though a mother of five may seem experienced and efficient and appears to handle her infant more competently, each baby has individual requirements. It takes time to learn what a particular baby's cries mean and what works best for us in mothering.

Adjusting to motherhood

Your abilities to adjust in the early days of motherhood are greatly affected by the level of support you receive in those first few weeks following birth. Early discharge from hospital is now a highly promoted option; many new mothers leave the hospital as early as 24 hours after an uncomplicated delivery.

It is not uncommon for mothers to say they received conflicting advice from maternity unit staff on feeding or handling their babies. This leaves mothers feeling confused and uncertain.

The best advice—and this applies in general to motherhood—is to listen to what people have to say if it interests you. If the advice seems sound, try it out; if it doesn't, don't worry about it. Above all, follow your instincts. When reading books about motherhood and parenting, use the same technique. As you get to know your baby better, you will learn what works best for him/her.

And so life changes...

The birth of the baby marks the end of the pregnancy and the true beginning of motherhood. And this is when life really changes!

The early weeks as a new mother are usually fairly hectic with little time for anything that does not involve your baby. While life is so baby-centered, it is the perfect time to reflect on your pregnancy and birth experience. It seems impossible to imagine now, but time does tend to cloud your memories of the experience somewhat—maybe this is nature's way of ensuring the human species survives!

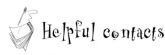

Helpful contacts

Maternity unit of your local hospital

The hospital where you gave birth may run groups where you can talk about your experience with other new mothers. If you participated in childbirth classes, keep in touch with others from your group, either formally or informally. Besides being a natural means of support, this can also lead to babysitting exchanges and playgroups when you and your baby are ready.

Domestic help

National Association of Postpartum Care Services — Can refer you to a certified postpartum doula (provider of all support services for new moms).
1 (800) 453-6852 (1 (800) 45-DOULA)
www.napcs.org

You can also look under "House Cleaning" in your local Yellow Pages.

Diaper services

Look under "Diaper Service" in your local Yellow Pages.

Circumcision information

American Academy of Pediatrics
1 (800) 433-9016
www.aap.org

NOCIRC (National Organization of Circumcision Information Resource Centers)
1 (415) 488-9883
www.nocirc.org

Grocery delivery

Some stores make home deliveries for a modest fee. Also, check out the online grocery delivery companies:

www.webvan.com (serving S.F. Bay area, Sacramento, Chicago and Atlanta areas)

www.homegrocer.com (serving Dallas/Ft. Worth, Los Angeles, Orange County, Portland, OR, San Diego and Seattle areas)

Birth Stories

http:www.geocities.com/Heartland/7269/

This site contains birth stories dating back more than twenty years and e-mail addresses for the authors. You can also contribute your own story.

Publications

There are several parenting magazines of interest to parents of infants and young children:

- *Parents*
- *Parenting*
- *Baby*
- *Child*
- *Working Mother*

Thoughts and feelings

Date: ....

- *The best thing about my pregnancy was …*
- *The worst thing about my pregnancy was …*
- *What I miss most about being pregnant is …*

....

....

....

....

....

....

....

....

....

....

....

....

....

....

....

....

....

Thoughts and feelings

Date: ....

- *If I had to sum up my baby's birth in one word, that word would be ...*
- *My experience of labor was ...*
- *Giving birth to my baby was ...*
- *Immediately after my baby was born, I felt ...*

21

Thoughts and feelings

Date: ....

- *What motherhood meant to me before my baby was born was ...*
- *What motherhood means to me now is ...*
- *When I hold my baby, I feel ...*

Thoughts and feelings

Date: ....

Thoughts and feelings

Date: ....

Thoughts and feelings

Date: ....

You might as well accept that your life will never be quite the same again but, then, would you really want it to be?

EISENBERG, HATHAWAY AND MURKOFF, *WHAT TO EXPECT THE FIRST YEAR*

chapter 2
Change, Transition, and Compromise

Changes to your body and mind, lifestyle, and relationships

Whether you deliver your baby in a hospital ward, in an operating theater or in a car—no matter where the birth occurs—the day comes when all new mothers bring their newborn home. This is often the time when gifts, flowers, and visitors begin to subside, but with a first baby, in particular, the applause can seem never ending.

Coming home is often when the reality of responsibility hits. Now there are no midwives or hospital staff on call if you are having difficulty with your baby settling in the middle of the night. Coming home is also when many new mothers truly begin to fall in love with their babies. Many women describe themselves at this stage as still being "on a high" from the birth, not because of drugs but because of the miracle of having their baby in their arms—at last!

Suddenly, you may feel that you don't know exactly what you're doing. Relax. You'll learn. There really is nothing like on-the-job training.

The changes brought about by your baby's arrival are complex. You will find yourself in perpetual transition alongside your baby as he/she grows from infant to toddler and beyond. You, too, will always be moving and changing. If you accept that change is inevitable, rather than resisting and struggling against it, you will find the transition to motherhood easier.

The pleasing punishment that women bear.
SHAKESPEARE

Body

Shape

One common complaint from mothers is that having a baby has changed the shape of their body. Despite returning to their pre-pregnancy weight following birth and exercising vigorously, the skirt of their favorite suit just doesn't fit any more. Probably no amount of dieting or exercising will change this. Many women welcome the changes, finding that having a baby has given them a more curvaceous, womanly figure.

Most mothers comment that their breasts have also changed. Though many think that breastfeeding is the cause of this, it is actually the changes that occur during pregnancy that alter the shape, and sometimes the direction, of breasts.

Size

Some women have difficulty losing the weight they gained during pregnancy. It takes nine months to make a baby and it will take at least that same amount of time to return to your pre-pregnancy weight. Of course, healthy eating and regular exercise will help to speed up the process.

Sweating

Those inconvenient hormones are to blame again here! Sweating is nature's way of helping to reduce the fluids in your body that may have built up during your pregnancy. Excessive sweating commonly occurs at night. When you are at rest, your body is very busy eliminating waste. It's one of those things that will subside with time, and there is little you can do about it. However, if the sweating is severe, it is best to consult your doctor or another health professional.

Hair loss

Your hair may change during pregnancy from dry to greasy or from slow growing to fast growing. Normal hair loss may also slow down for some women. Following birth, the hair that they would have lost during pregnancy begins to fall out. Sometimes the postnatal hair loss seems excessive. It will settle down over time. If the hair loss is causing you real concern, mention it to your doctor and to your hairdresser too.

Stress incontinence

Stress incontinence is the technical term for what happens if urine "escapes" when you cough, sneeze, or even laugh. It is usually only a temporary problem and is often resolved by doing pelvic floor exercises regularly.

It is common to have little feeling or sensation in your pelvic floor or to feel different in that region following childbirth. Pelvic floor exercises will assist in strengthening your muscles and will help you regain bladder control.

It helps to link these exercises with a regular daily activity so you are reminded to practice the exercises. Perhaps you could do them while feeding your baby or even while you are waiting at traffic lights!

Pull "up" and tighten the muscles you would use if you were trying to stop yourself from urinating. How many times can you do that before the contraction becomes weak? Repeat the exercises that number of times at least five times a day.

After about a week, check how many exercises you can now do consecutively before the contraction weakens. Increase number of exercises to that figure at least five times a day. There should be considerable improvement within a few weeks if the exercises are done properly and regularly. Consult your doctor or a physiotherapist if you have continuing problems with pelvic floor weakness.

Backache

Backache is commonplace following pregnancy and birth and is partly due to weakened abdominal muscles. Good posture certainly helps relieve and prevent backache. Ensure that you are seated comfortably and that your back is well supported when you are feeding your baby. When lifting your baby or anything for that matter, don't bend from your back, bend at the knees.

If your back is causing you discomfort or pain, contact your doctor or a health professional such as a chiropractor, physiotherapist, or osteopath.

The following postnatal exercise will help strengthen your abdominal muscles and support your back.

Lie on your back on a firm mattress or on a mat on the floor with your knees bent up and feet flat. With one hand on your stomach and the other hand under the small of your back, flatten your back onto your underneath hand, holding the position for a few seconds and then relaxing. Repeat this exercise 5–6 times, at least 3 times a day, progressing to a maximum of 20 times over the next fortnight.

Sexuality

Your sexuality may be considerably affected postnatally. Again, this varies for each individual. Some women experience no change at all. Whereas other women feel different after their birth experience. Some women's sexuality is enhanced by the changes brought about by pregnancy and birth. If you are experiencing difficulty with your sexuality as a result of your pregnancy and/or birth, contact your local doctor or obstetrician.

Mind

Memory

Many mothers admit to suffering from "maternal amnesia" in varying degrees. It most often starts in late pregnancy and is apparently caused by hormonal changes. Most women regain their memory once they have adjusted to the routines of looking after a baby. Breastfeeding mothers may find that the condition lasts longer.

Self-esteem and image

Your self-image may alter significantly after your baby arrives. You don't necessarily see yourself as you were before. You have changed, and you may find that difficult to accept.

Self-esteem can take a battering in the early months of motherhood if you do not ensure that your needs as a person are met.

Emotions

Emotions can run riot during pregnancy and beyond until your hormones have a chance to settle. There is nothing wrong with you. It may just take some time for your emotional balance to return.

Shift of focus

No matter what you say beforehand, your priorities will change after having a baby. Motherhood brings about a shift of focus, and life will never be quite the same again. Things that seemed important before your baby arrived are suddenly not nearly as significant. Many new mothers comment that they wonder what they did with their time before baby.

Different views on the world

With your baby's arrival, your view of the world may change. You may take far fewer risks. Things you would have done previously without thinking twice now require careful consideration. After all, you are now responsible for someone else.

More than likely, your thoughts will turn to the future. This is an appropriate time to consider consulting a financial planner, taking out life insurance, or preparing your will.

You may review your beliefs based on your new outlook on life and then take different stands than those you would have taken before. You may become passionate about issues that did not affect you previously. News items about babies and children that once you might have ignored, now jump out at you. You may not even be able to watch some movies that stir feelings within you.

Lifestyle

Restrictions on freedom

All of a sudden, those spur-of-the-moment decisions to go out are almost impossible. Given the amount of paraphernalia needed to get mobile with a baby in tow, it's surprising that new parents ever get out the door at all! Even outings planned with near military precision can be halted abruptly by an impromptu bout of crying or your baby's loaded diaper! In time, it really does get easier to get out and about. It just takes a little organization!

Sleep deprivation

Sleep deprivation is something you cannot understand until you have experienced it for yourself. It can leave you feeling anxious, on edge, and very irritable — not to mention totally exhausted, physically and mentally. If you are suffering from sleep deprivation and are having difficulty coping, speak to your local baby health nurse or the staff at a women's health center for some practical advice.

New opportunities

Having a baby presents you with many new opportunities: to extend friendships, to make new friends, to consider career choices, and to grow and develop on a personal level. Motherhood is eternally rewarding, often in the most surprising ways. The trick lies in seizing those opportunities as they present themselves.

Relationships

Partner

The arrival of your new baby brings inevitable, major changes to the status quo of your relationship with your partner—and this is largely beyond your control. It's not so much the changes to yourself and your partner but how you react to those changes that determines how your relationship will fare. It takes time for both of you to adjust to your new roles.

The strongest relationships are often put to the test after birth when the preexisting equilibrium is shaken or, in some cases, shattered. Happily, for most, the baby's arrival bonds the couple closer than before, cementing their relationship.

Emotionally

Emotions run high with a new baby, and this often exaggerates the whole spectrum of feelings. If you're happy, you're really happy. If you're sad, you're really sad.

It's crucial to try to keep the lines of communication open. Be direct and honest with each other at all times. It's very important that you pull together as a team so your life with baby can run as smoothly as possible.

You can't read your partner's mind so don't assume what your partner is thinking. He can't anticipate your thoughts or actions either. If you're having problems, share them. You are a team, a family. Solve your problems while they are still small and can be tackled easily. Minor problems can be blown way out of proportion if they are not dealt with promptly. Unexpressed negative emotions such as resentment can damage a relationship.

A lot of difficulties may be prevented if partners discuss what baby care and home duties each of them will do and set the ground rules before baby arrives. But it's never too late, of course, to figure these things out!

Jealousy is not uncommon, especially for partners who may feel that they've been forced out of the limelight by the new little bundle of joy. Well-wishers usually ask, "How is baby? And Mom?" They don't ask how your partner is! Breastfeeding can bring up feelings of jealousy and resentment for men who feel that mother and baby are bonding in a way that they never can. Mothers can also experience jealousy if they feel a lot of attention is being constantly lavished on baby while they are being ignored by their partner and others.

You may be so "in love" with your baby that you spend hours just adoring the infant—touching and cuddling, being with him/her. You may feel that you have little emotional energy to expend on your partner. He may, therefore, feel neglected. It's important that you continue to show him your feelings for him, even if it's only a hug before you fall asleep. Your partner needs to know that you still love him.

No emotion is right or wrong. If you are bothered by your feelings, talk it over with your partner. You may be surprised to find that he is not feeling 100 percent emotionally either. Becoming a parent, whether you are the one giving birth or not, is a time of major adjustment, and intense emotions are just one of the by-products of that process.

With the busy lives that we all lead these days, stress is common in and out of the home. Stress and strain in your relationship can be exacerbated by financial difficulties, differences of opinion, and many other factors. When baby makes three—or four or five—stress levels can go through the roof. You and your partner were committed to each other before the baby's birth. It's up to both of you now to ensure that the commitment endures. Some relationship counselors suggest that you and your partner make time daily to talk about anything except your offspring! So, set aside time for just the two of you to be a couple. Your baby and/or children are extensions of the bond you share. If you are having real communication problems, get some counseling. Take action now. Don't let things deteriorate.

Physically

When you will be ready to resume a sexual relationship is a contentious issue. Generally, doctors recommend that you wait until after you have been examined at your six-week postnatal checkup.

Feeling ready is a very individual, personal matter — which, again, may vary from your first baby to the second and beyond. It is decided by a whole host of factors: possible fear of pain from intercourse, fear of another pregnancy, a sense that your body is different, or altered self-esteem and self-image.

There are conflicting opinions as to whether breastfeeding your baby interferes with the return of your libido. Some "experts" say that breastfeeding may unconsciously satisfy your sexual needs and, therefore, you will be uninterested in a full sexual relationship with your partner. Others say that women who are breastfeeding resume their sexual relationships earlier than women who are not. Some partners may have difficulty with postnatal sexuality after seeing you physically endure the birthing process or they may be uncomfortable with breastfeeding.

Family

After your baby's birth, not only will you be adjusting to your new role as mother, there will also be changes in the status of your relationships with your extended family. You may discover a newfound respect for your parents or wonder why they did this or that when you were a baby.

If you are fortunate enough to have a good relationship with your mother, your voyage into motherhood may bond you even closer together. You may find, however, that your

We discover our parents when we become parents ourselves.

ANONYMOUS

family's opinions and views differ greatly from yours, and this may cause tension or conflict.

Other family members may have changed expectations of you now that you are a mother. Some may expect you to conform to their ideals. This can be extremely difficult to negotiate if their notions are fixed and entrenched. Be that as it may, this is your life and your baby. You need nobody's permission or authority to do what you believe to be best. Respect yourself and most other people will eventually respect you, whatever their initial views.

Friends

Sometimes the status quo of friendship is affected dramatically by your changed status. Your single friends may suddenly become unavailable. They may be uninterested in your new role or jealous or resentful. Even if they do stay involved in your life, you may find you haven't much to talk about for a while. They, quite naturally, will not be as enthusiastic as you are about your new baby.

Being a mother means finding a balance, reaching a compromise. Maintain friendships that really matter — friends who stick by you are the ones really worth the effort — and make new friends that include other mothers. This way, you get the best of both worlds. You still have a very real connection to friends with whom you have a history and who knew you before motherhood. Your new friends can share your baby's milestones and the ups and downs of parenting.

Others

Work associates and colleagues may change their image of you during your pregnancy and after you become a mother. Your pregnancy may have been threatening to some or, perhaps, you were perceived as becoming less competent than before. Some presume that you will simply return to work soon after giving birth, baby's arrival being little more than a hiccup in your career path, when you may intend to stay at home with your baby indefinitely.

Overall, people tend to project their ideas and voice their opinions on what is "right," no matter what you do. During this period of transition into motherhood, make choices that suit you—after all, you have to live with the outcome. If you, your partner, and your baby are happy with whatever it is you're doing, that is all that matters.

Having a baby changes you and so many facets of your life in the most wonderful ways, but some changes are easier to accommodate than others. The more established your career and the freer your lifestyle, the more profound the changes. Becoming a mother is much more than the physical act of childbearing. It is the ultimate transformation. There is nothing that compares.

Helpful contacts

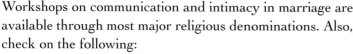

Workshops on communication and intimacy in marriage are available through most major religious denominations. Also, check on the following:

Association for Couples in
Marriage Enrichment
(800) 634-8325
www.marriageenrichment.com

Dr. John Gray seminars
(800) 821-3033
www.johngrayseminars.com
www.marsvenus.com

Dr. Harville Hendrix
seminars
(800) 729-1121
www.imagotherapy.com

You can also look in your local Yellow Pages under any of the following headings: "Clergy & Pastoral Counseling," "Family Planning Information Centers," "Marriage, Family & Child Counselors," "Mental Health Services," "Psychologists," "Psychotherapy," "Social & Human Services for Individuals & Families," and "Women's Organizations & Services."

Thoughts and feelings

Date: ....

• *How do you think your partner is feeling?*

Thoughts and feelings

Date: ....

- *Your moments of greatest joy are …*

_____

_____

_____

_____

_____

_____

_____

_____

_____

_____

_____

_____

_____

_____

_____

Thoughts and feelings

Date: ....

Thoughts and Feelings

Date: ....

....

....

....

....

....

....

....

....

....

....

....

....

....

....

....

....

....

....

Thoughts and feelings

Date: ....

The journey of a thousand miles must begin with a single step.
LAO TZU

chapter 3
It's All Right to Be Afraid

Coping with new emotions and responses: the joy and the fear

The learning curve

Don't be alarmed if, at first, you feel awkward attending to your baby or unsure of what you are doing. Learning the art of mothering can be difficult. It takes time to acquire the skills that you need. There is much trial and error—you learn as you go. This is especially true if you had little to do with babies before you had your own. Try not to worry. Do it at your own pace. Every day, over the weeks and months ahead, the tasks that you have to complete will become much easier and take far less time. Meeting your baby's needs will soon become second nature to you, and you will probably look back with some amusement on the early days.

Try not to set yourself up for disappointment with preconceived ideas of what you can, will, or should do. Failing to meet your own high standards and having idealized expectations of your ability to cope may damage your self-esteem. It will make your life a whole lot easier if you just go with the flow rather than having a definitive checklist of what you will do with a new baby. Aim for what you can realistically achieve.

Baby love

Loving your baby brings an intensity to your emotions. You will probably feel more passionately than you thought possible. This is perfectly natural and positive. Some mothers feel almost overwhelmed by the love that they feel for their baby. They could spend the day basking in the sheer joy that he/she has brought them, which is probably a good idea from time to time! Enjoy and savor the hours you have with your baby now because time goes quickly, and before you know it, you'll have a school-aged child on your hands.

It's not uncommon to be so protective of your baby that you have concerns over "what might happen if?" For example, there's barely a new mother around whose heart hasn't momentarily stopped when their newborn takes what seems like an eternity between breaths while sleeping.

Many women wonder what the future holds for their baby as he/she grows. The difficulty is that nobody knows what the future holds. Do your best as a parent and have faith that all will be well. There are many external influences and factors that we cannot control no matter how we try.

The emotional roller coaster

For many mothers, feeling fragile is not unusual in the first few months after birth, and those hormones are the culprits again! New mothers are vulnerable and may overreact to situations that would not normally faze them. Try not to worry too much. Put things in perspective. Look at situations from the outside. Keep your sense of humor.

Most new mothers feel low or miserable for brief periods of time or find themselves in tears on a bad day. If you are feeling like this a lot or are experiencing any of the following common symptoms, then you may be experiencing what is known as postnatal depression:

- crying excessively
- insomnia unrelated to meeting baby's needs
- overeating or undereating

- hyperactivity or constant lethargy
- withdrawal from usual behavior patterns
- difficulty making even simple decisions
- feeling overanxious and irritable
- feeling despondent or numb
- feelings of inadequacy
- feeling "out of control"

These symptoms describe common feelings in women with diagnosed postnatal depression. Some new mothers will feel some or all of these symptoms from time to time, yet they are just having difficulties adjusting to motherhood and require some support and/or counselling.

Tell your partner, a family member, or maybe a close friend how you are feeling and then make contact with your early childhood nurse, local doctor, or obstetrician for advice. They will be able to help you or to refer you to someone who can. It is important that you do this as soon as you can. The earlier you seek help, the easier the condition is to treat and the quicker the recovery.

Many intelligent, competent women find themselves "a mess" because they are unable, to meet their self-imposed standards, those implied by family tradition, and so on. The myths of motherhood, for example, suggest that: breastfeeding comes naturally and easily following birth; a mother instinctively knows why her baby is crying and how to comfort him/her; and a woman will receive complete satisfaction from the role of full-time mothering. Parenting is difficult enough without the stress of trying to live up to unrealistic standards. Set your own standards. Parent in the way that suits you best. Motherhood is not what many of us think it will be.

A good enough mother is good enough!

Be the best mother that you can be. There is no such thing as a perfect parent.

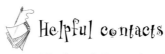# Helpful contacts

Mothers' Organizations

There are many helpful organizations designed to provide support and information to new moms, and the Internet is a great way to connect. Check on the following web sites:

www.babycenter.com (Baby Center)
www.parentcenter.com (Parent Center)

National Association of Mothers' Centers
(800) 645-3828
(516) 520-2929
www.motherscenter.org

You can also consult "Women's Organizations & Services" and "Crisis Intervention Services" in your local Yellow Pages.

Childcare

"Childcare Aware," a program of the National Association of Childcare Resource and Referral Agencies, can refer you to the appropriate local services.

 1 (800) 424-2246
www.childcareaware.org

National Child Care Information Center
(800) 616-2242
www.nccic.org

Partners in Delivering Quality Childcare
(877) 570-5437 ((877) 570-KIDS)
www.qualkids.com

Early Head Start National Resource Center
www.ehsnrc.org

Crisis

If you are having any difficulty dealing with your baby, or children, and feel unable to cope with the demands placed upon you, contact one of the following organizations who will be able to assist you with information, counseling, and appropriate assistance.

Parents Anonymous — for those feeling the stresses of parenting, this organization provides support and parenting skills. In addition to operating 24-hour hotlines, this group can direct you to local resources.
(909) 621-6184
www.parentsanonymous-natl.org
e-mail parentsanon@msn.com

Also, look under Crisis Intervention Service in your local Yellow Pages.

Nannies and Au Pairs

There are listings under "Nannies" in your local Yellow Pages. For assistance specifically with newborns, check under "Nurses & Nurse Registries."

There are also a number of websites devoted to nanny and au pair placement:
American Nanny Company
(800) 262-8771
www.AmericanNannyCompany.com

NaniNet
www.NannyNetwork.com
www.ParenthoodWeb.com

American Institute for Foreign Study
(800) 727-AIFS ((800) 727-2437)
www.aupairinamerica.com

Note: Be sure to check carefully before hiring any nanny.

For other support services, look in your local Yellow Pages under: "Birth & Parenting — Centers, Education & Services,"

"Child Care Centers," and "Child Care Consulting & Information Services."

Parenting Skills
Attachment Parenting International
(615) 298-4334
www.attachmentparenting.org

Postpartum Depression
Postpartum Support International — Support, education and local referrals for all postpartum resources, with a focus on mental health.
(805) 967-7636
www.postpartum.net

Postpartum Assistance for Mothers — Telephone support for both prenatal and postpartum anxiety and depression.
(510) 727-4610
www.postpartumassistance.com

National Association of Postpartum Care Services — referrals to certified postpartum doulas who provide support services.
 (800) 453-6852 (1 (800) 45-DOULA)
www.napcs.org

Also check out these web sites for information on depression:
www.depression.com
www.nmha.org (National Mental Health Association)

Thoughts and feelings

Date: ....

- *What I've learned so far about motherhood is …*

Thoughts and feelings

Date: ....

Thoughts and feelings

Date: ....

Thoughts and feelings

Date: ....

Thoughts and feelings

Date: ....

....

....

....

....

....

....

....

....

....

....

....

....

....

....

....

....

....

Thoughts and feelings

Date: ....

Thoughts and Feelings

Date: ....

Thoughts and feelings

Date: ....

A little of what you fancy does you good.

MARIE LLOYD (1879–1922), *ENGLISH ENTERTAINER*

chapter 4
Looking after You

Investing time in yourself

Time out for you

Being a mother is a challenging, rewarding, lifelong role. In the early weeks, especially, the rewards might seem few. It is easy to become so immersed in the day-to-day care of your new baby that you neglect yourself.

Mothers often put their babies' needs and those of other children and/or partners ahead of their own. This often appears to be the only option. Tending solely to baby's basic needs in the early months can take up at least 12 hours of the day!

The rewards of taking time to look after yourself are more than worthwhile:

- your spirits and energy level will be revitalized
- you will feel refreshed and be more focused
- you will be better able to care for your baby

A happy, more fulfilled mother usually means a happy baby and family. Here are some basic ways to help you care for yourself.

Regular meals and a balanced diet

Regular meals and a balanced diet keep your body operating at its most efficient. It is easy to skip meals and to eat on the run when you are busy. To ensure that you receive the vitamins, minerals, and nutrition you require, nutritionists recommend that you eat foods from the following food groups on a daily basis:

- one serving of meat or fish (beef, poultry, or seafood)
- two servings of milk and milk products (milk, yogurt, or cheese)
- three servings of fruit

Important telephone numbers

Mother

....

Best friend

....

Hairdresser

....

Beautician

....

Gym/fitness center

....

Masseuse

....

Baby-sitter

....

- four servings of vegetables
- five servings of bread and cereals (bread, pasta, cereal, or rice)

Fats, oils, and sugar should be consumed sparingly.

Essential routines

Exercise — Get out of the house every day, even if only for a 15-minute walk.

Beauty routine — Simplify your skincare routine and have an easy-to-care-for hairstyle.

Rest and sleep — Rest whenever you can. Recharging your batteries is important. Ask your partner or some other willing person to mind your baby while you sleep. Household chores will wait. Dust and clutter can be cleaned up fairly quickly and easily — fatigue accumulates rapidly.

Sharing the load — When someone offers you help, ask them to do something practical such as doing the dishes.

Boosting morale — If your self-confidence is at a low ebb, try to do something that makes you feel positive about yourself, something that makes you feel good.

Aromatherapy

Aromatherapy has become a widely accepted natural therapy that, among other things, uses essential oils to encourage relaxation. The purpose of aromatherapy is to rebalance the body, mind, and spirit.

Essential oils are powerful substances and should only be used as directed. They are usually absorbed into the body through massage, bathing, or inhalation. Apart from the therapeutic benefits of essential oils, they give pleasure through the senses of smell and touch.

Some oils are for general use; others have specific therapeutic benefits. For example, the oils used for relaxation are bergamot, clary sage, jasmine, lavender, rosewood, and ylang-ylang.

Oils vary in price and quality. Unlike cosmetics and skin-care products, where the most expensive brands are not necessarily the best, the price of essential oils is often in line with their quality. Some "oils" sold in supermarkets and other places are actually synthetic compounds that mimic essential oils, but do not have the same effects.

As a new mother, another pregnancy is probably the furthest thing from your mind, but note that some oils should be avoided during pregnancy. These include basil, clary sage, clove, cinnamon, hyssop, jasmine, juniper, marjoram, myrrh, sage, thyme, rosemary, fennel, and peppermint. If you are unsure, consult an aromatherapist or other specialist in the use of essential oils.

To gain the most benefit from aromatherapy, take full advantage of a quiet time when your baby is asleep or in the care of someone else. Run a warm bath and add the recommended drops of your chosen oil. Take the phone off the hook or switch on the answering machine. Hang a "Do Not Disturb" sign on the bathroom door. To add some atmosphere, put on your favorite music and light some candles. Get into the bath and relax.

Essential oil bath blends
Run your bath, then mix essential oils in 1 tablespoon of full cream milk, add to your bath, and agitate the water before soaking for 10–15 minutes.

Exercise
Regular exercise is essential. Don't underestimate the fatigue you will experience in the early months of motherhood, irrespective of the amount of sleep deprivation you might suffer. Ensure that you are sufficiently rested, and check with your doctor before you take up any vigorous exercise program.

Relaxing
3 drops lavender
2 drops orange
2 drops cedarwood

Soothing
1 drop orange
4 drops lavender
3 drops marjoram

Uplifting
3 drops pine
2 drops basil
2 drops bergamot

Revitalizing
3 drops rosemary
2 drops lemon
2 drops frankincense

Inspiring
4 drops basil
6 drops lemon
2 drops rosemary

Refreshing
2 drops bergamot
4 drops orange
6 drops frankincense

To maintain your current fitness level, exercise is generally recommended for at least 30 minutes at least 3 times a week. To help you lose weight, you will need to exercise for 30 minutes at least 4–5 times a week. Aerobic exercise, which raises the heartbeat and increases your metabolism and fitness levels, is required to help shift those excess pounds.

If you have no one to care for your baby while you exercise, remember that many health clubs and gyms provide child care during certain hours or class times. Contact your local gym to find out what they can offer you. That way you get both time out and exercise. Most gyms can tailor a comprehensive exercise program to suit your individual needs — whether you want to slim down or tone up.

You don't have to go to a gym. Any exercise that raises your heartbeat and keeps it elevated for a minimum of 20 minutes is termed "aerobic." It can be walking, cycling, swimming, jogging, dancing, rollerblading, etc. You will benefit far more from a short daily workout than from one long session weekly. Pop your baby into the stroller and head off. You'll both reap the benefits. There is really no excuse not to get up and go. Find a form of exercise that you truly enjoy, and you will be motivated to stick with it on a more permanent basis.

The following eight effective no-nonsense exercises can easily be fitted into a busy day and take a maximum of 20 minutes. Remember that you should warm up your body before you begin by walking briskly, marching on the spot, or maybe stationary cycling for at least 5 minutes. After doing the exercises, you should then cool down, using a similar technique to the one used to warm up.

1. **Bicep curl.** This exercise helps to tone and trim your upper arms. Hold a 2–4 pound weight (a can of food will do) in each hand. Stand with your arms by your sides. Without moving your elbow, lift one weight by bending your arm up until the weight is about 3 inches from your shoulder. Slowly lower the weight and return your arm to your side. Repeat the same exercise with the other arm. Repeat 20 times for each arm.

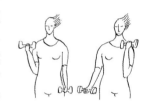

2. **Overhead press.** This exercise works the shoulders. Holding a 2–4 pound weight in each hand, stand and bend your arms so that your elbows are at shoulder level. Lift the weights by raising your arms above your head until your arms are extended fully. Lower both arms to shoulder height. Repeat 10 times.

3. **Lunge.** This exercise helps to tone and firm your bottom. Stand tall with feet together. Step your right leg forward into a lunge. Put all your weight onto your right leg. Ensure that your ankle and knee are in line. Push back to the starting position. Step your left leg forward into a lunge and repeat as above. Repeat 10 times for each leg.

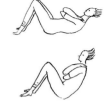

4. **Sit-ups.** With feet flat on the floor, lie down. Cross your arms over your chest. Focusing on your tummy, lift your shoulders off the floor, hold for the count of "two," then lower to the floor slowly. Do not use your neck or head for leverage. Inhale and tense your stomach muscles as you lift. Exhale and release your stomach muscles as you return to the floor. Repeat 20 times.

5. **Crunches.** This toning exercise is terrific for the tummy. Lie on your back on the floor. You can use a chair for support with your knees bent at about 90° if you need it. Cross your arms over your chest. Focusing on your stomach muscles, lift your shoulders up, aiming to reach your thigh. Do not use your neck or head for leverage. Inhale and tense your stomach muscles as you lift. Exhale and release your stomach muscles as you return to the floor. Repeat 20 times.

6. **Push-ups** (made easier!). A very effective upper arm toner; also great for your chest and shoulders. Lie on your stomach on the floor. Position yourself ready to push up — arms slightly forward, palms down, elbows close to your body. Keeping your knees on the ground and using your arms only, push up until your arms are almost straight. Lower yourself slowly to the floor. Repeat 20 times.

7. **Mule kick.** A great exercise for the bottom and legs. Position yourself on all fours, resting on your palms. Keeping your head in line with your body, lift your left knee toward your chest and, in one continuous, controlled movement, extend the leg behind you until it is straight. Return your left knee to the ground. Repeat with the right leg. Repeat for each leg 20 times.

8. **Bottom toner.** This is very effective for toning and firming your bottom. On all fours, leaning on your elbows for support, lift your right leg behind you, pushing your heel up toward the ceiling. Bring your right leg down in line with your body, at less than a 90° angle, and then push it up again. Repeat with the left leg. Repeat for each leg 20 times.

Massage

In the eastern world, massage has long been used to treat many different afflictions. It is only in recent years that the west has turned to massage as a therapy in areas other than sport. There are several types of massage techniques, including shiatsu, Swedish, holistic, and reflexology.

Massage has many benefits—physical, mental, and spiritual. It induces relaxation, relieves anxiety and tension, releases energy, and creates a sense of well-being. If you have never had a massage, this is something that you should organize today!

If that is not possible right now, you can feel some of the benefits of massage using the following do-it-yourself technique:

Work from feet to head. Start each body part with a light touch, working to a deeper, stronger pressure. Proceed slowly. Give yourself time to find out what feels best.

1. ***Legs and feet.*** Sitting on the floor, stretch your legs out in front of you. Working alternately from left to right, massage ankles, shins and calves, knees, and then thighs.

2. ***Back.*** Still sitting, massage your back, working up as far as you can, starting at your pelvis.

3. ***Hips and stomach.*** Lie down. Roll onto your left side. Work from the tailbone (coccyx), over your bottom, across your hip to your pelvic bone at the front. Roll over to your right side and repeat the process. Return to the floor, on your back, and massage your stomach.

4. **Chest.** Still lying, massage from your stomach to your neck. Working from the bottom up, massage between each rib from the middle outward.

5. **Arms and hands.** Still lying, massage each hand, forearm, elbow, upper arm, and shoulder, repeatedly alternating between the left and right side.

6. **Shoulders and neck.** While lying, massage the sides of your neck, pressing along the collarbone and shoulders. Massage the upper back as far as you are able.

7. **Face and scalp.** Still lying, firmly massage your face from the center outward, from your chin and jawbone to your forehead including your ears, then your whole scalp.

8. **Rest.** End the massage with rest.

Meditation

To meditate means "to turn within oneself." It is very much a personal journey, and it takes time to develop it as a skill. Reading books or taking classes about meditation can be worthwhile. It can set you on the path to improved health and deeper concentration and bring about an inner peace and sense of calm.

It is important to meditate daily, as regular meditation brings great benefits. You can start to meditate for as little as 5 minutes, progressing slowly to 45 minutes.

There are many methods of meditation. The method described below is one of the simplest techniques; it works on the basis of awareness of your breathing.

It is helpful to be able to relax completely before attempting meditation; however, that said, relaxation is one of the benefits of meditation!

- Find somewhere private, quiet, and warm where you will not be disturbed. Wear loose comfortable clothing. Some people enjoy background music that gives them a focus and seems to fade as they go deeper into the meditation. Others find music distracting. Experiment. See what works best for you. Like most things, if it feels good, do it. If it doesn't, don't!
- Sit on a cushion or in a chair with your back straight and well supported, and your hands in your lap, resting. Or lie on the floor with your head on a cushion for support. Consciously commit yourself to making the most of this time alone.
- Put your tongue at the back of your upper teeth and close your eyes. Focus your attention on the in-and-out movements of your breath, as it enters and leaves your nose or as your abdomen rises and falls. Breathe naturally but slowly. Count full breaths (in and out) from 1–10 over and over again. At first, you may be distracted by thoughts or sensations. Let go of those feelings by simply observing them and continuing to concentrate on your breathing or counting. This gets a lot easier with practice. Eventually your mind will be strengthened, and you will not be easily disturbed.
- After about 5 minutes, slowly bring yourself "back" into your environment. Open your eyes. Have a stretch. Stand up when you feel ready.

Life begets life. Energy creates energy. It is by spending oneself that one becomes rich.

SARAH BERNHARDT
(1844–1923), FRENCH ACTRESS

Relaxation techniques

Taking 20–30 minutes each day to relax has enormous benefits. Relaxation is a natural process that stills the body and the mind. It enables you to experience complete peace and calm, rare in a household with a baby and/or other children. Relaxation revitalizes you.

There are many varied procedures for relaxation, and the following simple method is only one of them. It is worth investigating the different techniques to see what is most effective for you.

- Set yourself up comfortably in a place where you will not be disturbed, at a time when you are not overtired or hungry.
- Lie on your back, arms at your sides, not touching your body. Keep your hands open and relaxed.
- Concentrating, inhale slowly and deeply saying to yourself or out loud, "I am calm." On the exhale say, "I am relaxed." Continue, and the deep relaxation breathing will eventually happen automatically. At first, your mind may wander and you may think about other things, but just return your thoughts to what you are doing and continue.
- You should eventually experience a sensation of heaviness—or some describe it as "lightness"—especially in your arms and legs.
- Focusing your attention on your feet, for example, notice sensations of fatigue and visualize any tightness in that specific area loosening.
- Proceed systematically from your feet to your head, focusing on each part, noticing the sensations of heaviness/lightness and visualizing an easing of any tension.
- If you have tension in a particular spot or a headache, focus on that body part and visualize warmth radiating into it. With practice, you may actually be able to feel a warm or tingling sensation as you do this.
- When you have completed this process, continue deep breathing. Say to yourself or out loud, with each alternate breath out, "I am calm," "I am relaxed."
- After a couple of minutes, return to deep breathing only. Gradually bring your consciousness back to the here and

now, becoming more aware of your surroundings with each breath. Open your eyes slowly and allow yourself a couple of moments to "wake up."

Once you have learned this technique, with regular practice, a state of complete relaxation will be easily achieved. You will then be aware of an obvious difference between feeling tense and feeling relaxed.

Go slowly. Be patient with yourself. It takes time to be able to relax. Unfortunately, in this day and age, most of us are tense more often than not. Some of us don't even realize how tense we are until we have learned to relax.

How beautiful it is to do nothing, and then rest afterward.

SPANISH PROVERB

Yoga

Yoga is an ancient exercise of the body, mind, and spirit. There are no prerequisite fitness levels. No special clothing or equipment is required. .

Some of the benefits of regular yoga include:
- strengthening and toning your body
- improved flexibility
- increased energy levels
- inner peace and outer calm

The Sun Salutation is a classic yoga sequence that can be done alone or as a warm-up in preparation for a yoga session. The 12 postures in the Sun Salutation stretch, tone, strengthen, and relax all the major muscle groups in your body. Build slowly until you can achieve the maximum of 12 repetitions of the sequence comfortably.

As with any form of exercise, start slowly and proceed gently. Don't force any stretches. As your body becomes more flexible through performing the sequence regularly, you will find that the stretches become easier. Hold each posture for 5 seconds then move to the next. The movements are meant to be fluid; one position flows into the next.

The Sun Salutation

1. Stand tall with your feet together and your hands together, as if praying. Breathe evenly and slowly.

2. Breathe in deeply as you raise both arms up over your head. With your neck relaxed and without straining, lean back slowly from your waist.

3. Breathe out as you bend forward from your hips, keeping knees slightly bent, and put your hands on your ankles or on the ground.

4. Breathe in as you move your left foot backward, keeping your knee in line with your toes on the ground. Keep your chin up.

5. Breathe out. Keeping your body and head in a straight line, take your right foot back in line with the left. Support your weight on your hands and toes. Look at the ground between your hands. Breathe in.

6. Breathe out. Gently lower your knees to the ground. Keeping your bottom up and your chin and chest to the ground. Toes should be curled under. Hands should be flat and elbows kept in close by your sides.

7. Breathe in. Raise yourself up by straightening your arms and lifting your chest off the ground. Toes should be pointing. Look up toward the sun.

8. Breathe out. Form a V shape with your body by placing feet flat on the floor, bottom up and arms straightened.

9. Breathe in. Return to the lunge position as in 4 above.

10. Breathe out. Bring your right foot forward as you bend from the waist, touching your ankles or the ground as in position 3 above.

11. Breathe in. Return to the position in 2 above with your arms raised, leaning back slowly from the waist.

12. Breathe out. Finish with hands praying. Gently lower your arms to your sides.

Other activities

Be social!

- Write a letter.
- Phone a friend.
- Have lunch at your favorite cafe without your baby.
- Have dinner at a restaurant.
- Ask a friend to go shopping or window-shopping.
- Join a club that you are interested in.
- Go to the movies, the theater, a concert, or to see a band.

Get creative!

- Paint or draw.
- Write poetry.
- Learn to play an instrument.
- Join a choir.
- Take photographs of subjects other than your baby.
- Practice your favorite craft — tapestry, knitting, sewing, woodwork, pottery.
- Join a woodworking class.

Get physical!

- Join a local sports team or take lessons in a sport you have always wanted to learn.
- Take dance classes.
- Go for a walk on your own.
- Take the dog for a walk.
- Go to the gym and work out.
- Do some gardening.
- Do yoga or tai chi.

Get educated!

- Enroll in an educational course or study group.
- Listen to audiotapes to learn a new language.
- Take time to do a crossword puzzle.
- Go to the library and lose yourself in books.
- Visit a museum or an art gallery.

Get in touch with you!

- Meditate.
- Do yoga or tai chi.
- Relax in a warm bath.
- Fill in some note pages in this book.
- Listen to some relaxation tapes and just empty your mind.

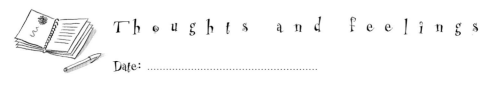

Thoughts and feelings

Date: ....

- *What I miss doing is …*
- *I feel good when I …*

....

....

....

....

....

....

....

....

....

....

....

....

....

....

....

....

....

Thoughts and feelings

Date: ....

Thoughts and feelings

Date: ....

....

....

....

....

....

....

....

....

....

....

....

....

....

....

....

....

....

Thoughts and feelings

Date: ....

And when you're tempted to feel guilty about asking for help,
remind yourself that you've been working all day too.

EISENBERG, HATHAWAY AND MURKOFF, *WHAT TO EXPECT THE FIRST YEAR*

chapter 5

Establishing a Support Network

Sharing the load – how others can help

Where does support come from?

Your experience of the early weeks of motherhood can be considerably affected by the level of assistance and support you receive. In western society, there are generally no formal rituals to support women who have recently given birth. In some other countries and cultures, relatives and friends rally around the new mother for a considerable time. They basically take over the care of her partner, other children if she has any, and the running of the home, allowing the new mother to rest, recover, and get to know her newborn baby.

Not so long ago, a western family was a tighter knit, closely bound unit, supported and surrounded by relatives, who all lived within close proximity and usually remained there for most of their lives. Only a generation or two ago, families were generally larger, and older children helped with the care of the younger ones. When you had your first baby, your mother or older sister was on hand to ease your transition to motherhood, providing much-needed guidance and practical assistance. There was a sense of rapport in the community. Neighbors would often cook meals for new mothers and offer a helping hand when it was needed.

Many changes have enabled us to live in ways that would not have been possible years ago. With advances in technology and transportation, we have been able to move to distant places, to climb the corporate ladder, or to follow a career path, usually leaving our family of origin behind in another state or even another country. Consequently, we sometimes find ourselves cut off or isolated.

Establishing a support network is one of the most effective ways of making your life easier. It does not only mean having people around you that you can rely on for baby-sitting or household help. An effective support network also provides you with a web of information, advice, contacts, and many other things.

So who do you turn to for support when you are a new mother?

Your partner

If you have a partner, you are in the position of having someone to share the journey with. You and your partner can support each other mutually in many ways. You have someone who can become actively involved in baby's everyday care, thereby freeing you for personal time. You also have someone to talk to, to bounce ideas off, and to participate with you in the trials and tribulations of parenting.

Your partner cannot always be there, so you need backup support. This ensures that there is someone else you can rely on in a crisis. You also need to spend some time with your partner alone.

Family and friends

If you are fortunate enough to have members of your family who are willing and able to be a real part of you and your baby's life, then you have access to a wonderful source of support.

Friends can also be a significant part of your support network. They can provide much in the way of practical help and be a source of encouragement and solace. If your friends are parents themselves, then that makes an ideal exchange system of information, suggestions, and maybe even baby-sitting.

Other new parents

As a mother with a new baby, there are many opportunities for meeting others in a similar situation.

Joining or forming a playgroup can be a real lifesaver, particularly during the first year or so of motherhood. Much can be gained from these groups—you will meet others with children of similar ages and find that you are not alone in your struggles or concerns. You will make new friends and acquaintances, learn a lot about parenting, share information and tips, and have a good laugh. Your baby will also benefit greatly from these get-togethers, particularly as he/she grows and starts to interact with others. Playgroups usually meet on a weekly basis and provide companionship, play, and support. Parents may establish independent playgroups.

Whether you join a playgroup or whether you meet up with just one other new parent, having other parents as part of your support network is extremely beneficial. Having someone to listen to you who understands what you are talking about is sometimes the best form of support one could wish for.

Attend your next class reunion if one has been arranged. There, you can be assured of meeting up with other new parents with babies close in age to yours. Many firm friendships are founded at these reunions. Some parents continue to get together on a regular basis with their babies. As time goes on, second and sometimes subsequent children are often born at around the same time as those of your friends, forming an extended network of families.

Many communities have a local child resource center. They should be able to provide information regarding playgroups, classes, talks and discussion groups, and mother and baby groups available in your immediate area. Don't forget the nearest park or playground!

Baby and toddler exercise classes

Physical activity classes such as Gymboree are a fun way for your baby to develop many skills. These classes are usually held on a weekly basis for about an hour. Led by professional staff, the classes give your baby the opportunity to play and learn and actively involve you in activities with your baby. The classes also give you the chance to meet other mothers with infants around the same age as your little one.

Your local church

Your local church may have special meetings or times set aside for parents and their babies and/or children. Maybe they run an informal playgroup or have tea and coffee mornings for new mothers. Get in touch and find out what they have to offer.

Baby health nurses

Baby health nurses who carry out routine screening and examinations play an important role in your young baby's life. They also provide a wealth of information and practical advice relating to the early years of motherhood. Your physical and emotional well-being is of importance to these nurses, and they are available to talk to you about relevant issues or to refer you to someone more appropriate in the circumstances. Your local child resource center is often a good meeting point for new mothers.

Women's health centers, walk-in clinics, and residential units

There are numerous centers for new mothers that provide assistance. If you are having feeding or sleeping difficulties with your baby or if you need other support, they should be able to help you. Many centers and other organizations also run clinics and specific classes for new parents.

Surrogate grandparents

If you have no family within easy reach, you can always adopt a family. There are many elderly people in the United States and Canada, some of whom are isolated from their own adult children by distance. Surrogate grandparents can enrich your baby's life, and they gain much personal satisfaction from interacting with you and your baby and feeling needed themselves.

Sharing the load

Chore	Me	Partner	Share	Outside help
Cooking				
Shopping				
Vacuuming				
Washing				
Ironing				
Bathing baby				
Night shift				

Helpful contacts

Breastfeeding Support

Ask your pediatrician for a list of volunteer or professional breastfeeding counselors in your area, or contact:

 National Association of Postpartum Care Services
1 (800) 453-6852 (1 (800) 45-DOULA)
www.napcs.org

La Leche League — Toll-free number provides immediate consultations Monday through Friday from 9 a.m. to 5 p.m. Central time.
1 (800) LALECHE
After hours, or if the (800) line is busy, try the automated "locator service" at (847) 519-7730 for a referral to the 24-hour volunteer who is currently on call in your local area.
www.lalecheleague.org

 Breastfeeding National Network — for breastfeeding products and for referrals to lactation consultants in your local area.
1 (800) 835-5968; 1 (800) TELLYOU
www.medela.com

International Lactation Consultant Association — can provide referrals to local lactation consultants.
(919) 787-5181
www.ilca.org

Special Supplemental Nutrition Program for Women, Infants and Children (WIC). See your phone book or contact your local Health Department.

Support for Multiple Births
National Organization of Mothers of Twins Clubs
(877) 540-2200
www.nomotc.org

Center for Study of Multiple Birth
(312) 266-9093

www.multiplebirth.com

Mother and Child Activities
Parent-infant play classes are available in most areas; look in your phone directory or check with your local community center or religious institution. You can also contact your local YMCA, which offers Early Head Start programs for children three months and older (under the federally funded Head Start program).

Single Parents
Parents Without Partners
(561) 391-8833
www.parentswithoutpartners.org

Browse the Internet
http://www.childbirth.org/aftercare.html

This is a discussion group by e-mail covering all aspects of motherhood.

http://www.storksite.com/
This site is an on-line support network for parents.

Thoughts and feelings

Date: ....

Thoughts and feelings

Date: ....

YESTERDAY AND TOMORROW

There are only two days in every week about which we should not worry:
two days which should be kept free from fear and apprehension.
One of these days is YESTERDAY *with its mistakes and cares,*
its faults and blunders, its aches and pains.
YESTERDAY *has passed forever beyond our control.*
All the money in the world cannot bring back YESTERDAY.
We cannot undo a single act we performed,
we cannot erase a single word we said.
YESTERDAY *is gone.*
The other day we should not worry about is TOMORROW
with its possible adversities, its burdens,
its large promise and poor performance.
TOMORROW *is beyond our immediate control.*
TOMORROW'S *sun will rise, either in splendor*
or behind a mask of clouds — but it will rise.
Until it does, we have no stake in TOMORROW,
for it is yet unborn.
This leaves only one day — TODAY.
Any man can fight the battles of just one day.
It is only when you add the burdens of those two awful eternities —
YESTERDAY *and* TOMORROW *— that we break down.*
It is not the experience of today that drives men mad —
it is remorse and bitterness for something which happened YESTERDAY
and the dread of what TOMORROW *may bring.*
LET US THEREFORE LIVE BUT ONE DAY AT A TIME.

SOURCE UNKNOWN

chapter 6
The Superwoman Syndrome

Stay-at-home mom, career woman, or both?

To work or not to work

Whether you choose to stay at home and care for your baby, or whether you choose to work outside the home and have your baby cared for by someone else, you are more than likely going to be working harder and longer hours than ever before. You will also probably be more fulfilled than you have ever been! Being a mother is always a 24-hour-a-day role—whether you stay at home or are in paid employment.

Some women must return to the workforce shortly after giving birth due to financial constraints but would rather, given the chance, be at home with their babies. Others feel pressure to stay at home on a full-time basis when they actually need the mental stimulation of work.

None of us is in a position to judge another on the issue of working mothers. There is no right way. The best way is your way!

At the end of each day, mothers at home often feel that they have achieved little if anything, although they have fed and changed their babies as often as required and attended to all their other needs. These include stimulating their offspring with toys and conversation, giving them affection, putting them to sleep, pacifying them when they're distressed, washing or ironing clothes, cleaning or tidying the home, and perhaps shopping and preparing an evening meal! Despite their best efforts, things do not always go as planned and mothers at home often feel guilty that they are not contributing to the family's income.

On the other hand, mothers who work outside the home, whether by choice or necessity, may feel that

Jugglers aren't paid very well, and sometimes they get hit on the head with the balls they have in the air.
ANONYMOUS

they should be at home with their babies, particularly if they are ill or teething. They might feel guilty that they're missing their babies' first attempts at crawling or their first words. They could also be reluctant to admit that they actually look forward to going to work each day and enjoy it while they are there.

With love, care, and the right environment, babies are fairly adaptable. When it comes down to it, if you do have a choice, you must do what is right for you because that will usually be what is best for your baby. For example, some mothers would much rather be employed outside the home for personal reasons, which include adult contact, a sense of achievement, and financial and personal autonomy. If you are happy in whatever you do, usually your family will be too.

These days, with a greater level of flexibility in employment, most women have a number of choices regarding work and raising a family. You may find that after your baby is born and your return to work is imminent, your priorities have changed and you do not wish to return to paid work. Alternatively, your time at home with your baby so far, although it has been wonderful, may have left you feeling isolated and itching to get back to work for your own personal satisfaction.

Returning to or starting full-time employment requires careful forethought. There are questions that require your consideration before you start work.

- Why are you considering going to work?
- Do the benefits outweigh the costs?
- Are you satisfied with the proposed childcare arrangements?
- Do you have the support of your partner and/or family — who will do what at home? What contingency plans can you set in place in case of an unforeseen emergency? How are you going to manage your time effectively so you can balance work and home life?
- How flexible is your employer?

- Is part-time or flex-time work an option?
- Is a phased or staged return to work possible for you so your childcare arrangements for drop-offs and pick-ups are more flexible in the early days?

For most women returning to full-time employment, the benefits of working do outweigh the costs, but don't underestimate the difficulties of trying to balance home and work life. You are likely to be very tired at times, and your baby will succumb to a few minor ailments—coughs, colds, and viral infections—in the first year or two. Some employers are more accommodating than others when it comes to taking time off to nurse a sick child. This is something you should broach when negotiating your return to work or a new job.

You will certainly need to ensure that you have your support network firmly fixed in place for use in times of need. If you have a partner, talk about your shared responsibilities in relation to the care of your baby and domestic duties.

There are several alternatives to full-time employment, which include:
- part-time employment including job sharing, flextime, and term time
- telecommuting
- self-employment from home or outside the home

Part-time employment

Working on a part-time basis enables you to enjoy the best of both worlds. There are many advantages to this kind of working arrangement for both you and your employer. Among other things, you are able to spend a reasonable amount of time caring for your baby while earning an income and maintaining continuity of employment. Part-time employees save employers time and money in advertising and training.

Job sharing

Job sharing is now a fairly common option for employees, particularly working mothers. Job sharing enables two or more people to share a salary, job benefits, and work space.

Flextime

Flexibility in working hours makes it is easier to juggle work and home commitments. You may be able to change your hours by starting earlier or leaving later than usual, according to need. Most companies will require that you work certain core hours, for example, 10:00 A.M. to 3:00 P.M.

Telecommuting

Advances in technology and communications mean there are now many office jobs that can be carried out mostly from home. If it is possible to convince your employer that you need not physically be in the office every day, then telecommuting may solve your working dilemma. Working from home enables you to look after your baby much of the time, although someone to care for him/her while you are attending to your work duties is still necessary. Basic equipment for this arrangement would include a computer with a modem, a telephone, and a facsimile machine. Telecommuting allows you to spend less time and energy traveling to and from your place of employment. You and your employer should negotiate which day or days you are needed at your workplace.

Self-employment

Many people dream of having a business of their own. Some of the main advantages of self-employment include:
• being able to structure your own working hours

- being your own boss
- having more control over your finances and your life

Many new businesses fail within their first two years because of lack of planning and management skills. Success requires discipline, dedication, and ambition.

The fastest growth sector of small business in the United States and Canada is the home-based business. A larger and larger percentage of self-employed people operate their business in their home or their business is based at home. Growth is believed to be escalating as a result of technological advances in communications.

Self-employment, whether home-based or outside the home, gives you greater flexibility in childcare arrangements. Depending on the type of business, most self-employed mothers, except possibly those who work during the evenings, require some form of childcare during their working hours in order to work efficiently and professionally.

Being self-employed enables you to have time with your baby and the satisfaction of pursuing your chosen career.

She never quite leaves her children at home, even when she doesn't take them along.
MARGARET CULKIN
BANNING

Breastfeeding

Breastfeeding your baby is possible even when you return to the workforce. Your early childhood nurse can provide you with the necessary supporting information to assist with this. Some mothers decide to wean their baby before returning to work. Other express breast milk at intervals during the day, which is fed to their babies by their caretakers.

Childcare

Quality care for your baby is one of the most important factors in deciding to return to work. You will need to investigate your childcare options.

Family or relatives

You may be fortunate enough to have a family member who volunteers to take care of your baby while you work. This will save you a lot of money compared with what you would pay for care in a formal childcare setting and will ensure your baby has continuity of care.

Family day care

These caretakers operate from their own homes. In the United States and Canada, there are formal requirements for family day-care centers. Those requirements can vary from location to location. They usually require a certain level of training and a proven commitment to the welfare of children.

One of the advantages of home-based care is that the groups of babies or children are small.

Au pairs

Au pairs are predominantly young women from overseas who are in the United States or Canada to study and learn English. They undertake most domestic duties including childcare. Au pairs are unlikely to have childcare or formal qualifications.

Nannies

Nannies are generally qualified to care for children and, although they are mostly young, they usually have some experience. If you cannot find one recommended by someone that you know and trust, you should choose a reputable agency to help you find a suitable nanny. A day nanny visits the home on a daily basis during set hours. Nannies can also live in. There is no set wage for a nanny. The wage is a matter for you and the nanny to agree upon.

Day-care centers or preschools

Preschools or day-care centers are usually run by qualified and trained staff. Untrained assistants may also work there. Licensing covers safety, sanitation, caretaker's qualifications, and the number of children allowed to be cared for on the premises. Licensing does not cover quality of care. In all cases, day-care centers or preschools should be evaluated for their standard of care and their licensure.

The age ranges and numbers of children in day-care centers or preschools vary considerably. Groups are usually larger than those looked after by home-based caretakers; however, the day-care centers or preschools generally have structured programs to meet the developmental, physical, and emotional needs of the babies and children in their care. The day-care centers or preschools operate for set hours with set fees. Inquire whether financial assistance is available from your local preschool or day-care center.

Workplace childcare

Workplace childcare enables employees to have their baby cared for within or very close to their workplace. This makes drop-offs and pick-ups easier at the beginning and end of each working day. You may also be able to pop in during a break to check on your little one.

It's up to you

When going back to work, do what you can to pave the way for a smooth transition. These are some of the more important things to remember:

Organize — Establish routines. Keep a journal. Make lists.

Prioritize — What is important or essential? What is not?

Delegate — Who can take on some of the domestic duties? What else can others do?

Network — Talk to other mothers in similar situations. Their support will be invaluable.

Despite a busy schedule, you will have to carve out some time for yourself. You have needs and desires, too, and rights as your own person. Don't try to do everything yourself. Put the Superwoman cape away; it's better to be good enough than to struggle to achieve unattainable perfection.

Motherhood is a potential minefield of guilt. No matter which way you go, someone is bound to criticize you or attempt to undermine your decisions. This is why it's really important that you are confident in your choice and your roles. Change your mind if you realize that what you're doing doesn't work for you. Don't be swayed into feeling that you ought to be doing something else. Don't feel guilty. If it's not a problem for you, then it's simply not a problem.

Helpful contacts

There are many organizations dealing with motherhood and employment choices.

Home-Based Working Moms
(512) 266-0900
www.hbwm.com

Online network for moms at home in business:
www.momsnetwork.com

Working Moms Refuge
www.momsrefuge.com

Working Mother magazine website:
www.workingwoman.com

Formerly Employed Mothers at the Leading Edge (FEMALE)
Mothers and More
(630) 941-3553
www.femalehome.org

Mothers At Home
(703) 352-1072
www.mah.org

National Association for the Self-Employed
(800) 232-6273
www.nase.org

For other business resources, check under "Women's Organizations & Services" in your local Yellow Pages.

Small Business Administration (SBA)
See under "Small Business" in the business section of your local White Pages.

Family Daycare Training

Childcare Aware, a program of the National Association of Childcare Resource and Referral Agencies.

1 (800) 424-2246

www.childcareaware.org

National Association for Family Child Care

(515) 282-8192

www.nafcc.org

Also, look under "Child Care Consulting & Information Services" in your local Yellow Pages.

Decision to work

Use this chart to help you when planning your proposed return to work.

For	Against
Working will bring me an income.	A percentage of my income will be spent on childcare costs.

Thoughts and feelings

Date: ....

Thoughts and feelings

Date: ....

_____

_____

_____

_____

_____

_____

_____

_____

_____

_____

_____

_____

_____

_____

_____

_____

_____

Thoughts and feelings

Date: ....

Thoughts and feelings

Date: ....

Thoughts and feelings

Date: ....

_____

_____

_____

_____

_____

_____

_____

_____

_____

_____

_____

_____

_____

_____

_____

_____

Mothers are real people, too.

ANONYMOUS

chapter 7
Survival Kit

Making life easier

If there's ever a time in your life that you will need a survival kit, it's when you become a mother. Many women have commented that having children means never being able to go to the bathroom alone again; never relaxing during a phone call; never getting to finish a cup of tea or coffee while it is still hot. And these changes, for most, are just the tip of the iceberg!

Personal qualities

Given the challenges and rewards that lie ahead of you, you will need to develop the following attributes.

Acceptance—Accepting the changes to your life that will accompany the arrival of your baby makes it much easier to cope with the transition to motherhood.

Tolerance—Bear with yourself, your partner, and others as you adjust to your new roles in parenthood.

Humor—Try to see the funny side of situations. Even more important than being able to laugh at situations is the ability to laugh at yourself.

Patience—Be patient—with your partner, your baby, and especially with yourself.

Other important matters

Reliable contraception

Unless you would welcome another pregnancy, it is vital that you use reliable contraception.

Time out

You were with your partner before your baby was born, and it is now important to be nurturing in the relationship as before. It can be damaging to a relationship to see each other only as parents, rather than as the individuals that you still are and as partners in a relationship. Baby can only benefit from a mother and father who have a fairly healthy, generally happy relationship with each other. Taking time out for the two of you as a couple is essential for the well-being of your relationship and, ultimately, your family. A strong relationship between parents is a solid foundation for a family.

That said, however, you are an individual. You have your needs and wants too and, provided that your baby's needs are taken care of, you have the right to have them satisfied. The word "mother" will not mean "martyr" unless you act like one! Whether you need your partner to take care of baby while you go for your morning walk or whether you need to work full-time for whatever reason, you will be a far happier mother if you are reasonably satisfied. Your growing baby will see you as a woman who has her own needs and who is respected because she respects herself enough to satisfy those needs.

Reasonable time out, time away from baby, is not only recommended for you, it's also good for baby. Baby learns to cope with other caretakers, adjust to a different routine, and cope with new situations. Babies are generally flexible little beings who can handle being without mom quite well for short periods of time. It's often mom who cannot bear to be away from her little one for too long!

There are many ways you can make your life easier after you have your baby—as with most things, you get out what you put in.

Housekeeping

When it comes to housekeeping, it is best to aim for easy and hygienic, rather than spotless and sterile! Do only what is essential, especially in the first weeks after your baby is born.

If finances permit, pay someone to do things for you. If you're unable to do this, accept offers from all those who ask, "Is there anything I can do?" Let friends and relatives wash the kitchen floor, do the vacuuming, do the dishes, help with the ironing, and so on.

Shopping

Plan ahead. Consider shopping fortnightly or even monthly. If you have a willing partner, or caretaker, consider shopping at night—many major shopping centers are open late and some all night. It's also a chance to get some baby-free time. If that's not an option, some vendors will take phone orders and home deliver. Take advantage of such services.

Cooking

There are ways to make this daily chore easier. Even those of us who love to cook can find that juggling a tired, grizzly baby and cooking the evening meal can be difficult.

- Cook double portions, and freeze the extra portion for another meal.
- Prepare lunches the night before, or even better, early in the week for you, your baby, other children, and your partner. It may seem like a lot of effort at the time, but you will be amazed at how much time it saves you daily.
- Make friends with your microwave and your freezer. They are instrumental in helping you save time and energy in preparing the family's meals.
- Prepare and precook dinner earlier in the day, and reheat it in the microwave when you're ready to eat.

Quick and easy meals

Vegetable soup

Puree cooked vegetables in the blender or food processor. Thin the puree with water, stock, milk, or cream. Reheat and serve. Top with croutons, a little grated cheese or a swirl of cream for something different.

Ham and pumpkin soup

Makes about 1 quart.

Ingredients

2/3 cup ham, chopped finely

1/2 small pumpkin (butternut is good), seeds and skin removed

1 small onion, chopped finely

1 quart chicken stock

2 teaspoons butter or margarine

Cream

Method

1. Cut pumpkin into bite-size pieces.
2. Melt butter/margarine in large saucepan.
3. Saute onion until it browns lightly.
4. Add ham and pumpkin, stir until well mixed.
5. Add stock and bring to a boil. Then reduce heat and simmer for 20–30 minutes. Allow to cool.
6. Blend the soup in a food processor until completely smooth.
7. Reheat and serve immediately with cream to taste.
8. Refrigerate overnight in an airtight container for up to five days or freeze in meal-size portions. To defrost, use a saucepan over low heat or microwave.

Cajun prawns and salad
Serves 2

Ingredients
1 pound cooked prawns
Cajun spice mix
Medium cucumber, sliced on the diagonal
1 pint cherry tomatoes
Lettuce
Medium Spanish onion, sliced

Method
1. Toss lettuce, onion, cucumber, and tomatoes in a salad bowl.
2. Place the prawns on a foil-covered tray.
3. Sprinkle the prawns with the spice mix.
4. Heat the prawns in a slow oven for about 5 minutes then serve with the salad.

Casserole
Serves 4

Ingredients
1 pound trimmed steak (round preferably), cut into small strips
1 onion, chopped
1 garlic clove, crushed
Olive oil
2 carrots, sliced
2 celery stalks, sliced
6 button mushrooms, halved
1 can chopped tomatoes with juice
1/2 cup red wine
Fresh bay leaf
Lemon rind, grated
1 teaspoon mixed (fresh or dried) herbs
1 tablespoon cornstarch

Method
1. Cook onion and garlic over high heat, in oil, until onion browns.
2. Add meat, stir and cook until browned.
3. Add tomatoes, juice, wine, bay leaf, herbs, lemon rind, and all vegetables except the mushrooms. Bring to a boil.
4. Reduce heat. Mix in cornstarch.
5. Cover and simmer for 1 1/2 hours or until meat is tender.
6. Add mushrooms to the casserole about 10 minutes before the meal is cooked.
7. Serve with steamed rice or small new potatoes.

Chicken stir-fry
Serves 4

Ingredients
4 skinless chicken breast fillets, chopped into bite-size pieces
1 clove garlic, crushed
5 spring onions, chopped finely
1 red and 1 green sweet bell pepper, sliced
1 cup snow peas
1 cup broccoli
2 tablespoons mild sweet chili sauce (optional)
4 tablespoons tomato puree
3 cups of long-grain rice, steamed

Method
1. Heat a wok or frying pan over high heat. Add garlic and onions. Sauté.
2. Add chicken and stir until it is all white.
3. Stir in tomato puree and chili sauce.
4. Add peppers, broccoli, and snow peas. Stir-fry for 3–4 minutes until vegetables are slightly tender.
5. Serve with hot steamed rice.

Fruit brûlée
Serves 4

Ingredients
1 cup natural yogurt
1 cup fromage frais (any flavor)
2 cups of pineapple, sliced (retain the juice from the can)
5 fruit-filled cookies chopped into bite-sized pieces
1 tablespoon raw sugar

Method
1. Place half of the cookie pieces and pineapple juice into large bowl.
2. Add half of the pineapple pieces.
3. Top with half of the serving of fromage frais and yogurt.
4. Add the remaining cookie pieces and pineapple.
5. Top with the remaining fromage frais and yogurt.
6. Sprinkle with sugar and serve.

Fruit cocktail
Serves 4

Ingredients
1 pint strawberries, pureed
2 kiwi fruit, chopped
1 large orange, chopped
1 can of sliced pineapple
1 large can of mixed fruit

Method
1. Cut orange, pineapple, and kiwi fruit into bite-size pieces and place into a large bowl.
2. Mix thoroughly.
3. Add mixed fruit and stir.
4. Top with pureed strawberries and serve chilled.

Escaping the home

Have a small bag packed with the bare essentials for your baby: a couple of diapers, a change of clothes, and a few toys. Pack only what you need for a couple of hours. Refill the bag soon after you return home, or the next time you run out the door, you won't have the essentials you might need!

Traveling

All babies become accustomed to traveling by some means or another. For most of us, traveling by car or on public transportation—by train, bus, or ferry—is a daily event.

Some mothers travel frequently by air. There are many ways to make long-distance air travel easier with baby in tow.

- Check ahead with your airline or travel provider to see what they have to offer to assist parents.
- Pack a bag of essentials to keep with you for the duration of your trip. A small selection of favorite toys is important.
- Take one toy out of your bag at a time; otherwise, your baby will play with everything at once and soon get bored.
- If you are traveling abroad, try to book a flight for the early evening so you have a better chance of getting your baby to sleep for a considerable part of the flight.

Baby-sitting

Having some time out occasionally without baby is a real necessity, but leaving your baby in someone else's care, even in your own home, can be difficult. Most new mothers feel that nobody can take care of their baby as well as they can. Remember how important it is that you nurture yourself by having time away, even for just a couple of hours every few weeks.

If you don't have access to a willing family member, then the next best thing is a baby-sitter who comes recommended by a trusted friend or from a baby-sitting agency. When hiring a baby-sitter, make sure that his/her background and references have been thoroughly checked.

Baby-sitting co-op

A popular alternative is a baby-sitting co-op where parents join together to provide mutual baby-sitting. Generally, a co-op begins with a small group of parents who all know and like each other. Other parents join by members' recommendation. Rules should be agreed on for the foundation of the group, such as when and how the hours you baby-sit will be repaid. A baby-sitting co-op is a good idea as it can cost nothing and you know your baby-sitter has had personal experience.

As a mother, remember to . . .

- Enjoy the time that you share with your baby. Take the opportunity to just be together. It really is the quality of the time that you spend with your baby that matters.
- Listen to the pearls of wisdom that other people give you if it interests you. If the advice seems sound, try it out. If it doesn't sound right or it's something you don't agree with, disregard it.
- Make choices that suit you. If you and your baby and your partner are happy with whatever it is you are doing, then that is all that really matters.
- Nurture yourself. A more fulfilled, happier mother generally means a happy baby and family.
- Feel positive about your choice to return to work or to stay at home. If it's not a problem for you, it's just not a problem.
- Choose your own mothering style; there is no right way. The best way for you is your way!

Thoughts and feelings

Date: ....

Thoughts and feelings

Date: ....

....

....

....

....

....

....

....

....

....

....

....

....

....

....

....

....

....

Thoughts and feelings

Date: ....

Thoughts and feelings

Date: ....

....

....

....

....

....

....

....

....

....

....

....

....

....

....

....

....

....

....

Thoughts and feelings

Date: ....

Thoughts and feelings

Date: ....

_____

_____

_____

_____

_____

_____

_____

_____

_____

_____

_____

_____

_____

_____

_____

_____

_____

_____

Thoughts and feelings

Date: ....

Suggested Further Reading

Barrett, Nina (1997) *I Wish Someone Had Told Me: A Realistic Guide to Early Motherhood*, Academy Chicago Publishers.

Bing, Elisabeth and Colman, Libby (1997) *Laughter and Tears: The Emotional Life of New Mothers*, Owlet

Burkett, Wynn McClenahan (2000) *Life After Baby: From Professional Woman to Beginner Parent*, Wildcat Canyon Press

Eisenberg, Hathaway and Murkoff (1991) *What to Expect the First Year*, HarperCollins. (These authors have a series of book from pregnancy to the toddler years and all are highly recommended reading.)

Kelly, Marguerite, et. al. (1975) *The Mother's Almanac*, Doubleday

Lamott, Anne (1994) *Operating Instructions: A Journal of my Son's First Year*, Fawcett Books

Lazear, Jonathon & Wendy (1993) *Meditations For Parents Who Do Too Much*, Simon & Schuster.

Rich, Adrienne (1995) *Of Woman Born: Motherhood as Experience and Institution*, W.W. Norton & Company